OF NATURAL HEALING

HAJAR YOUNG

Copyright © 2017 by Hajar Young
All rights reserved.

This book or any portion thereof may not be reproduced or used in any manner whatsoever without the express written permission of the publisher except for the use of brief quotations in a book review.

Printed in the United States of America
First Printing, 2017

ISBN 978-1-942674-20-7

Table of Contents

Disclaimer and Terms of Use Agreement	2
Acknowledgements	3
Introduction	4
What is Illness	5
What is Disease	5
The Stomach is our Second Brain	6
Integrative Consciousness — The Need to Heal the Attitude	6
Meridian Tapping Therapy	7
Hajdrienne Technique	7
What are Body Meridians	7
Massage Therapy	8
Physical and Mental Benefits of Massage (Bodywork)	9
Meditation and Prayer	10
Inflammation	11
Essential Oils	12
How to Use Essential Oils	13
Herbs	21
Supplements	27
Remedies from Your Kitchen	30
Honey and Cinnamon	30
Spice It Up	42
Ayurveda	44
Oil Pulling	44
Worst Foods to Consume	45
Sugar	45
High Fructose Corn Syrup	47
Fat, Salt And Sugar Alter Brain Chemistry	49
International Flavors and Fragrances, Inc.	50
Alkaline Water	51
Cupping	52
Breathing	52
Benefits of Proper Breathing	54
Sun Gazing	54
Benefits of Sun Gazing	56
Mac's Home Remedies	57
About the Author	59
Personal Movement	60

DISCLAIMER AND TERMS OF USE AGREEMENT

Nothing in this document is intended to constitute medical advice or treatment. Information in this document is a combination of information found in medical literature and information acquired through personal observation by Hajar Young. This information is for informational purposes only. Because there is always some risk involved, the author of this document is not responsible for any consequences resulting from the use of any suggestions or procedures described in this document. Please check with your doctor or nutritionist before making any dietary changes. If you wish to apply ideas contained in this document, you are taking full responsibility for your actions. The author and publisher shall in no event be held liable to any party for any direct, indirect, punitive, special, incidental or other consequential damages arising directly or indirectly from any use of this material, which is provided "as is", and without warranties. All links are for information purposes only and are not warranted for content, accuracy or any other implied or explicit purpose.

Acknowledgements

The Presence of God makes all things possible. I begin In The Name and Presence of God.

My moral support to complete this book came from my dearest friends, Dr. Adrienne Sabir, Majeedah Rashada, Amina Ali, and Khaleelah Shabazz.

The African American Advisory Council of the Reparatory Theatre of San Diego shared my confidence that I could fulfill a need in the community by making this book available.

This book is dedicated to my daughter Khadijah Robinson and her daughter Suhialah Robinson. They are my motivation to keep striving with a positive presence. I pray my sincere and loving counsel to both these young women, as well as to my seven other grandchildren, whom I love so dearly, has influenced their spirituality and maturity. They each are a work of art in progress. "I saw an angel in the marble and carved until I set it free", Michelangelo.

And to both my sons who support me in all my ventures and adventures.

Thank you Mac Curtis for lending me some of your tried and true remedies.

Edited by Frances A. Walls

Introduction

Americans spent over $374 BILLION dollars on prescriptions in 2014. They filled 4.3 billion prescriptions. The data shows that American's spending on medicine hit the highest level since 2001, up 13% in 2014 compared with the year before, according to data from the IMS Institute for Healthcare Informatics. Per person, we spend 40% more than any other nation on healthcare.

Current estimates are that it may cost as much as over a billion dollars to develop a drug by a pharmaceutical company. Today's magic bullets or targeted therapies are expensive as cost of treating advanced colorectal cancer patient that was $500 in 2006 is $250,000 just ten years later as indicated by Leonard Saltz, from Memorial Sloan-Kettering Cancer Center, New York. Despite billions that have been spent, the death rate from most cancers has barely budged.

If you take into account the amount spent in the entire medical industry the number is simply staggering: $3.8 Trillion dollars.

That's more than the entire Gross Domestic Product for 87% of the countries of the world! And yet, despite spending all that money, America is still ranked 17th in terms of quality of health.

What is Illness

What if we not consider illness our enemy, to be rectified with drugs, but rather, see it as an event, a mechanism of the body, that is serving to cleanse, purify and balance us on the physical, emotional, mental and spiritual planes.

Our bodies are outward signs of inward consciousness, just as a painting is the visible expression of an artist's ideas. Our bodies, in fact our whole lives, are nothing other than a reflection of our spiritual situation.

This book will bring forth some "natural remedies" to balance/heal our mind, body and spirit and facilitate new perspectives concerning our health conditions.

What is Disease

Disease is defined as "A particular pathological condition that affects a part, or all of an organ, or system of an organism resulting from various causes, such as infection, genetic defect, or environmental stress, and characterized by an identifiable group of signs or symptoms."

It has become customary of most human beings to believe that dis-ease is a part of our daily lives. I feel that the state of our mind, as well as our spirit, is what needs to receive attention, when the body is challenged by a state of disease. Disease is not a natural state of being.

With that in focus, addressing the metaphysical cause, utilizing nutrition (for mind and body), breathing, visualization, balancing, body cleansing, immune activation and support, clean water, gratitude, prayer, silence, touch, massage, laughter and love, (especially love of self) all are utilized to correct imbalances. There is a probable mental pattern behind the diseases of our bodies; most often fear and anger. Begin the practice of replacing fear and anger with love. Flow/live in the rhythm of love. All things have a vibrational frequency. Our Universe has a rhythm. Feel the vibrations of Mother Nature. Smell and ingest the vibrational energy of herbs and essential oils. Experience *The Wonders of Natural Healing*.

The Stomach is our Second Brain

The strongest of us are likely to experience that familiar feeling of "butterflies" in the stomach. Underlying this sensation is an often-overlooked network of neurons lining our guts that is so extensive some scientists have nicknamed it our "second brain".

A deeper understanding of this mass of neural tissue, filled with important neurotransmitters, is revealing that it does much more than merely handle digestion or inflict the occasional nervous pang. The little brain in our innards, in connection with the big one in our skulls, partly determines our mental state and plays key roles in certain diseases throughout the body.

Integrative Consciousness –
The Need to Heal the Attitude

There is a new medical model which says diseases like cancer are not just the result of diet, genetics and environmental toxins. Disease is thought to be the result of unexpected trauma which registers on the psyche, a particular part of the brain and in an associated organ or part of the body. For every physical condition experienced there is a metaphysical component.

To cure the disease we must resolve the trauma. When the trauma is resolved, the body starts an automatic healing process.

MERIDIAN TAPPING THERAPY (NEEDLELESS ACUPUNCTURE)

Hajdrienne Technique

MTT is an abbreviation for Meridian Tapping Therapy. MTT is based on the assumption that negative emotions disrupt the flow of the body's energy system. When energy patterns are disrupted due to physical, mental or emotional trauma, it is believed that the path of energy between neurons is disrupted. Tapping on meridian points on the body, derived from ancient acupuncture practices, can release energy blockages that cause negative emotions leading to disease. We are moving further and further away from basic techniques for healing ourselves, organic within us and in nature. There are a variety of techniques and innovations that incorporate body meridian point tapping. This is a technique which I and my colleague, Dr. Adrienne Sabir, incorporate into our stress management consultation practice. It includes deep breathing, MTT, aromatherapy and massage. This procedure is called the *Hajdrienne Technique*.

What are Body Meridians

Body Meridians are energy channels 'transporting' life energy (Chi/Qi) throughout the body. If there are blockages, leading to lack of energy supply to certain areas of the body, or a surplus of energy in other areas, imbalances occur.

Energy blockages can be the result of stress, an injury or trauma, or bad living habits (diet, addictions, lack of exercise) and can be traced to the root of all health (physical, mental, spiritual) problems.

Our energy flow affects how we feel, how we think, and the overall condition of our health situation. When the body's life-force energy becomes blocked, various imbalances will result.

For centuries, in China, Japan, Tibet, India and other countries, life has been considered as a bio-electrical/vibrational energy phenomenon.

It is only because of the existence of this energy in our body that we can move, breathe, digest food... think and even feel.

Different cultures call this energy by different names... 'Prana', 'Chetana' or 'Qi' (Chi).

Qi is composed of two kinds of forces: 'Yin' and 'Yang'. A person remains in good health if there is harmony and balance between these two forces.

If the balance is disturbed, that is, if the flow of one of these forces is greater than the other, illness arises. These forces – energies – flow through definite channels in the body, called 'body meridians' (body's healing energy pathways).

Most Meridian Tapping Techniques involve saying certain phrases that identify a personal aggravation, ailment, or life situation which can help you focus and heal those issues. The phrase will end as thus, "I deeply and completely love and forgive myself". There are 8 or 9 tapping points. You can use two fingers to touch and tap on the meridian points yourself, or someone can tap on them for you. A MTT professional can help you learn the correct tapping points as well as guide you through a tapping sequence (or 'round' as they are commonly called) and assist you in saying phrases that will be of most benefit. The *Hajdrienne Technique* releases negative emotions and energy flows uninterrupted again.

John Dewey: *"The self is not something ready-made, but something in continuous formation through choice of action."*

MASSAGE THERAPY

It is necessary to ask how a society such as the U.S., which is so technologically advanced and civilized in appearance, can be simultaneously so violent and unsuccessful in interpersonal and intercultural relations. Studies in the area of touch are providing some answers for those who wish to listen. Virtually everyone has an intense need to be held and soothed and stimulated, but we find ourselves receptive at relatively brief moments in our lives.

We tend to be touched less and less as we get older, although our primal need for touch never diminishes. Touch deprivation is a significant form of sensory deprivation. Most of us wouldn't dream of going weeks or months without opening our eyes or keeping our ears plugged, yet many of my clients tell me that they haven't been massaged or held for weeks or months.

Healthy touch from another human being slows your heart rate, decreases the levels of cortisol in your system, and eases anxiety. It's no wonder that touch is so important.

For the sake of your physical, emotionally, mental and spiritual health, give yourself more permission to touch and be touched. You can never overdose on loving touch. Everyone needs a hug. It is fat-free, sugar-free and it relieves pain and depression.

Don't limit touch to sex. Don't limit touch to just your partner and family. Reach out and touch more people. You'd be surprised to find outgoing socialites who long to be hugged.

Our world is becoming too formal, too stiff, and too emotionally cold. Close your eyes sometimes and experience your world through touch.

Massage therapy is a form of touch. It is the manual manipulation of soft body tissues (muscles, connective tissues, tendons and ligaments) to enhance a person's health and well-being. There are dozens of types of massage therapy methods (also called modalities).

Physical and Mental Benefits of Massage (Bodywork)

- loosens tight muscles
- relieves tired and aching muscles
- increases flexibility and range of motion
- diminishes chronic pain

- calms the nervous system
- lowers blood pressure
- lowers heart rate
- enhances skin tone
- assists in recovery from injuries and illnesses
- strengthens the immune system
- reduces tension headaches
- reduces mental stress
- improves concentration
- promotes restful sleep
- aids in mental relaxation
- relaxes the whole body

Carl Jung: *"The meeting of two personalities is like the contact of two chemical substances: if there is any reaction, both are transformed."*

MEDITATION and PRAYER

Meditation has not only spiritual benefit but worldly benefit, and can be a means for healing and finding creative solutions to difficult problems. Meditation is one of the most important aspects of a successful and healthy lifestyle.

Dr. Wayne Dyer reminds us that, "Perhaps the most elusive space for human beings to enter is the gap between our thoughts. When you attempt to **clear your mind,** usually the act of clearing your mind only leads to more thoughts.

Usually we stay on one thought until another one takes over, leaving very little unused space. The spaces between our thoughts are brief, and seldom does anyone wonder what it would be like to have fewer thoughts or what we'd find in the void between them".

Take time to meditate. Meditation is difficult for many people because their thoughts are always on some distant object or place. One form of meditation is to label the thought as it appears and then choose to let it go. This practice helps you first become aware of your thoughts, which many of us need to do, so that we can return to the present moment.

Prayer takes concentration. It is an act of meditation. Clear your mind and take an intimate and inward turn utterly towards God. Contemplate on your invocation, ponder. Concentrate on what you are saying. Don't just imitate others. Healing is taking place in this moment.

Muhammad, The Prophet: *"Do you know what is better than charity and fasting and prayer? It is keeping peace and good relations between people, as quarrels and bad feeling destroy mankind."*

INFLAMMATION

Inflammation is the body's attempt at self-protection; the aim being to remove harmful stimuli, including damaged cells, irritants, or pathogens - and begin the healing process.

When something harmful or irritating affects a part of our body, there is a biological response to try to remove it, the signs and symptoms of inflammation, specifically acute inflammation, show that the body is trying to heal itself.

Inflammation does not mean infection, even when an infection causes inflammation. Infection is caused by a bacterium, virus or fungus, while inflammation is the body's response to it.

Chronic inflammation can eventually cause several diseases and conditions, including some cancers, rheumatoid arthritis, atherosclerosis, periodontitis, and hay fever. Although scientists know that inflammation plays a key role in heart disease and several other illnesses, what drives inflammation in the first place is still a mystery.

It should be remembered that inflammation is part of the healing process. Sometimes reducing inflammation is necessary, but not always.

The immune system communicates directly with the nervous system and affects important health-related behaviors such as depression. This scientific finding could bring relief to patients afflicted with obesity, which leads to chronic inflammation, as well as to cancer patients treated with radiation and chemotherapy drugs that produce both inflammation and depression.

Include plenty of these anti-inflammatory foods in your diet:
- tomatoes
- olive oil
- green leafy vegetables, such as spinach, moranga, and collards
- nuts like almonds and walnut.
- fatty fish like salmon, mackerel, tuna, and sardines
- fruits such as strawberries, blueberries, cherries, and oranges

ESSENTIAL OILS

The most powerful forms of healing are found right here on God's green earth. Mother Nature knows more than humans will ever know. And she provides everything we could ever need to maintain vibrant health well into our mature years.

Essential oils are part of today's natural miracle remedies. The practice of using essential oils has been around for thousands of years. You can consider essential oils as the "life blood" of a plant. They circulate through all the plant tissue and carry nutrition into the cells and waste products out. Thus, the "essential" part... without them, the plant would die!

When high quality essential oils are applied to your skin, they do many of the same tasks as they do while inside the plant. They quickly permeate the cell walls of your skin to deliver nutrition and remove waste. As they do this, they help to clean the receptor sites of your cells... receptors that are easily disrupted by heavy metals and petrochemicals (the chemicals found in plastic).

This cleansing effect helps to restore balance to your body, which ultimately helps you to feel better.

How to Use Essential Oils

There are really only three basic ways:
1. Aromatherapy
2. Topical Application
3. Ingestion*

*CAUTION: Not all essential oils are ingestible and some may be poisonous.

Black Seed Oil - Primary Benefits

Black Seed (Nigella sativa) is likely the most scientifically studied essential oil. The Black seeds are small black grains with a rough surface and an oily white interior, similar to onion seeds. The seeds have little bouquet, though when rubbed, their aroma resembles oregano. They have a slightly bitter, peppery flavor and a crunchy texture.

The Black Seed is also known by other names, varying between places. Some call it black caraway; others call it black cumin, onion seeds or even coriander seeds. Although it is commonly referred to as black cumin, the plant has no relation to the common kitchen herb, cumin.

Nigella sativa is actually a different plant than black cumin. Black cumin has different properties from black seed and shouldn't be confused.

It is said that the Black Seed Oil is a remedy for everything except death. Black seed oil, in fact, was found in Egyptian Pharaoh Tutankhamen's tomb, dating back approximately 3,300 years. Many of Black Seed Oil's traditionally ascribed health benefits have been thoroughly confirmed in the biomedical literature. Since 1964, there have been 656 published, peer-reviewed studies referencing it. To insure that you are taking the Black Seed look for the words Nigella Sativa. Only this plant, as opposed to true cumin or coriander has the ability to "heal all diseases."

Black seed has been researched for very specific health conditions. Some of the most compelling applications include:

- **Type 2 Diabetes:** Two grams of Black seeds a day resulted in reduced fasting glucose, decreased insulin resistance, increased beta-cell function, and reduced glycosylated hemoglobin (HbA1c) in human subjects.
- **Helicobacter Pylori Infection:** Black seeds possess clinically useful anti-H. Pylori activity, comparable to triple eradication therapy.
- **Epilepsy:** Black seeds were traditionally known to have anticonvulsive properties. A 2007 study with epileptic children, whose condition was nonresponsive to conventional drug treatment, found that a water extract of Black seeds significantly reduced seizure activity.
- **High Blood pressure:** The daily use of 100 and 200 mg of Black seed extract, twice daily, for 2 months, was found to have a blood pressure-lowering effect in patients with mild hypertension.
- **Asthma**: A study in human subjects, found that boiled water extracts of Black seed have relatively potent anti-asthmatic effect.
- **Acute tonsillopharyngitis:** Black seed capsules have been found to significantly alleviate throat pain and reduce the need for pain-killers.
- **Chemical Weapons Injury:** A randomized, placebo-controlled human study of chemical weapons injured patients found that boiled water extracts of Black seed reduced respiratory symptoms, chest wheezing, and pulmonary function test values, as well as reduced the need for drug treatment.
- **Colon Cancer:** Cell studies have found that Black seed extract compares favorably to the chemo agent 5-fluoruracil in the suppression of colon cancer growth, but with a far higher safety profile.

- **Opiate Addiction/Withdrawal:** A study on 35 opiate addicts found Black seed an effective therapy in long-term treatment of opioid dependence.

Cinnamon Bark Oil – Primary Benefits

Cinnamon Bark Oil is an extremely powerful anti bacterial. Cinnamon Bark Oil is effective against 65 strains of antibiotic resistant bacteria.

Other benefits of Cinnamon Bark Oil are:
- Supports healthy metabolic function
- Maintains a healthy immune system
- Flavors food
- Repels insects naturally

Dilute cinnamon oil with water to disinfect kitchen counter tops, sinks, your refrigerator, door knobs, toys and many other things. If you have young children and don't want to use harsh cancer causing chemicals use Cinnamon Oil. If you want a mild disinfectant, to wash your face, then a couple of Cinnamon sticks boiled in hot water might be an idea.

Echinacea Oil – Primary Benefits

Also known as purple coneflower, Echinacea is a classic medicine that is used to strengthen the immune system, fight infections and fever. Ecnchincea essential oil also is used as an antiseptic and general treatment for colds, cough and flu.

Other health benefits of Echinacea include:
- Boost the immune system,
- Eliminate bacterial and viral infections
- Reduce inflammation
- Improve skin conditions like eczema and psoriasis

- Protect respiratory health
- Prevent recurrent infections like ear infections

Eucalyptus Oil - Primary Benefits

The oil from the leaves and roots of Eucalyptus is a common treatment when infused in a tea to treat coughs, sore-throat, flu and fever. Eucalyptus is used to this day as an ingredient in cough drops.

Eucalyptus Oil also has these benefits:
- Assists with cleaning bad breath
- Supports overall respiratory health
- Soothes tired, sore muscles
- Effective in treating sinusitis

Frankincense Oil - Primary Benefits

Use Frankincense Oil as preventative measure against oral health problems such as bad breath, toothaches, cavities, canker sores, and other infections. Try mixing with baking soda and coconut oil to make your own toothpaste.

Frankincense Oil can be used with these benefits:
- Cleans and cares for distressed skin
- Relieves restless leg syndrome when applied to the bottom of the feet
- Supports immune function
- Removes moles, skin tags, and warts

Lavender Oil - Primary Benefits

Lavender has been used for over 2,500 years. Ancient Persians, Greeks, and Africans added the flowers to their bathwater to help wash and purify their skin. In fact, the word "lavender" comes from the Latin word "lavare," which means "to wash."

Phoenicians, Arabians, and Egyptians used lavender as a perfume, as well as for mummification — mummies were wrapped in lavender-dipped garments.

In Greece and Rome, it was used as an all-around cure, while in Medieval and Renaissance Europe, it was scattered all over stone castle floors as a natural disinfectant and deodorant.

Lavender Oil can be used to:
- Calm and relax the mind
- Soothe occasional skin irritations
- Help skin conditions recover quickly
- Ease muscle tension

Lemon Oil - Primary Benefits

Lemon oil is calming in nature and therefore helps in removing mental fatigue, exhaustion, dizziness, anxiety and nervous tension. It has the ability to refresh the mind by creating a positive mindset and removing negative emotions. It is also believed that inhaling lemon oil helps in increasing concentration and alertness. It can therefore be used as a room freshener in offices to increase the efficiency of the employees.

Lemon oil has a high vitamin content, which makes it a wonderful booster for the body's immune system. It further stimulates white blood cells, thus increasing your ability to fight off diseases. Lemon oil also improves circulation throughout the body.

Other benefits of Lemon include:
- Cleansing and purification
- Oral health and remedy for halitosis (bad breath)
- Thirst quencher
- Remedy for abdominal colic pain
- Cough relief
- Calms stomach and relieves nausea
- Improves digestion
- Nourishes the skin
- Promotes Weight loss

Marjoram Oil – Primary Benefits

Marjoram essential oil is helpful in curing nearly all types of spasms and related problems. It efficiently relieves spasm in the respiratory system and intestines, and muscular spasms in the limbs. It also helps to control convulsions, pulled muscles, cramps, and spasmodic cholera that are caused from uncontrollable spasms.

Marjoram essential oil helps to suppress or control sexual desires. This property is beneficial for those who are suffering from abnormal and extreme sexual urges.

Marjoram Oil is used to:
- Provide relief from stress and anxiety
- Aid in curing viral and bacterial infections
- Protect wounds from becoming septic

Oregano Oil – Primary Benefits

The disinfectant and antibacterial properties of oregano essential oil were first recognized in ancient Greece where they were often used for treating bacterial infections on the skin or in wounds, and it was also employed to protect food from bacteria. It is a plant native to higher altitudes and normally grows in the mountains, which is how it got the name "Oregano", which means "Delight of the Mountains".

Other benefits of Oregano Oil:
- Immune support
- Apply to bottom of feet as a natural defense against infection
- Use internally as a part of a monthly cleansing regimen
- Use for Gastro Intestinal health

Peppermint Oil – Primary Benefits

The health benefits of peppermint oil include its ability to treat indigestion, respiratory problems, headache, nausea, fever, stomach and bowel spasms, as well as for pain relief. Due to the presence of menthol, menthone and menthyl esters, peppermint and peppermint oil find wide applications in the manufacturing of soap, shampoo, cigarettes, toothpaste, chewing gum, tea and ice cream.

Peppermint is a cross between watermint and spearmint and is native to Europe. Historically, the herb has been known for its medicinal uses, and its impressively long history often gives it the prestigious title as the world's oldest medicine.

Peppermint Oil also:
- Promotes healthy respiratory function
- Encrgizing and cooling aroma
- Use in toothpaste and chewing gum for oral health
- Alleviates occasional stomach upset

Tea Tree Oil - Primary Benefits

Tea tree oil is applied to the skin (used topically) for infections such as acne, fungal infections of the nails, lice, scabies, athlete's foot, and ringworm. It is also used topically as a local antiseptic for cuts and abrasions, for burns, insect bites and stings, boils, vaginal infections, recurrent herpes, toothache, infections of the mouth and nose and sore throat.

Some people add it to bath water to treat cough, bronchial congestion, and pulmonary inflammation. The chemicals in tea tree oil may kill bacteria and fungus, and reduce allergic skin reactions.

Other uses for Tea Tree Oil include:
- Use for ear infections
- Apply to skin blemishes
- Use with shampoo and conditioner for healthy scalp and hair

Wild Orange Oil - Primary Benefits

Possibly one of the most distinct characteristics of Wild Orange essential oil is its powerful scent. The strong, sweet, citrus aroma of Wild Orange makes it useful for purifying the air, promoting and energizing an uplifting environment, or simply creating a pleasant smell in the home. To harness the purifying power and aroma of Wild Orange essential oil, place a few drops on your air filter at home. This will improve your home's scent while simultaneously purifying the air.

Wild Orange Oil also has these benefits:
- Protects against environmental and seasonal threats such as cold and flu.
- Immune-enhancing qualities
- Energizing and revitalizing to the mind and body

Wintergreen Oil - Primary Benefits

The oil of wintergreen is a world famous name, and it is extremely popular with the people suffering from rheumatism, arthritis, gout and pain in their bones and joints from any number of reasons. This oil can usually be found in every household.

Wintergreen Oil has many additional applications:
- Promotes blood circulation and cools irritation
- Soothes achy muscles and joints
- Promotes healthy respiratory function
- Relieves headaches and chronic nerve pain
- Reduces symptoms of PMS and arthritis.

Ylang Ylang Oil - Primary Benefits

Derived from unique star-shaped flowers, Ylang Ylang is often used to support healthy skin and hair, while simultaneously providing a calming effect and promoting a positive outlook.

Ylang Ylang Oil has these benefits:
- Helps balance hormones
- Lifts mood
- Fights parasites
- Regulates heartbeat

"Behave so the aroma of your actions may enhance the general sweetness of the atmosphere." Henry David Thoreau

HERBS

An herb is any plant with leaves, seeds, or flowers used for flavoring and seasoning of food, medicine, or perfume.

Alfalfa:
Alfalfa relieves digestion and is used to aid blood clotting. Contemporary uses include treatment of arthritis, bladder and kidney conditions. Alfalfa strengthens the bones and enhances the immune system.

Aloe Vera:

Aloe-Vera is a cactus-like plant. The thick leaves can be squeezed to extrude a thick sap that can be used to treat burns, insect bites and wounds.

Bee pollen:

When mixed with food bee pollen can boost energy, aid digestion and enhance the immune system. If you're allergic to bee stings you will most likely be allergic to bee pollen.

Bees Wax:

Bees Wax is used as a salve for burns and insect bites, including bee stings. Bees Wax is intended to only be used externally.

Blackberry:

The root, bark and leaves of Blackberry when crushed and infused in a tea are used to treat diarrhea, reduce inflammation and stimulate the metabolism. As a gargle it treats sore throats, mouth ulcers and inflammation of the gums.

Buckwheat:

The seeds of Buckwheat are used in soups and as porridge to lower blood pressure, help with blood clotting and relieve diarrhea.

Chamomile:

The leaves and flowers of Chamomile are used as a tea to treat intestinal problems and nausea. Chamomile is a gentle herb known throughout most of the world which has been used continually for many centuries. It is often ingested as a tea to calm the nervous system and the digestive tract, and is mild enough to be administered to babies with colic. Chamomile is soothing to irritated skin and membranes, and is often found in lotions and hair products. Other studies illuminate this plant's potential to assist in healing wounds and soothing gastrointestinal conditions.

Comfrey:

Genus name for Comfrey is *Symphytum*, which means to "unite or knit together." The name com-firma means simply "knitting of bones. You can use the leaf and the root, fresh or dried.

Comfrey contains a special substance called allantoin, which is a cell proliferative. In other words, it makes cells grow faster. This is one of the reasons why comfrey-treated bones knit so fast, wounds mend so quickly and burns heal with such little scarring.

This same substance, allantoin, is found in the placenta of a pregnant mother which helps the baby grow rapidly. After the baby is born, allantoin is also found in the mother's milk — abundantly at first and less so as the child grows. Comfrey is rich in vitamin B12, which is important to vegetarians, as very few plants have B12. It is also rich in vitamins B1, B2, C, E, A and pantothenic acid plus calcium, iron, manganese and phosphorus.

Dandelion root extract:

Dandelion Root is found to kill leukemia cells, prostate cancer cells and chemo-resistant melanoma. Chemo-resistant melanoma is now the most common type of cancer affecting Americans aged 25 to 29. The only option doctors can presently offer these patients is surgery to remove the tumor and its surroundings, followed by immunotherapy, which does not usually work when the melanoma has metastasized.

However, all that looks set to change, thanks to a humble plant that many people pull out of their gardens and throw away. Dandelion root extract can cause human melanoma cells to essentially kill themselves without leading to any type of toxicity. In fact, studies showed cancer cells disintegrating within 48 hours, while healthy cells remained unaffected. The benefits of dandelions don't end there. The root can also stimulate the secretion of bile, relieve allergies, reduce cholesterol and cleanse the liver. In addition, Dandelion root contains high amounts of Vitamin A and Vitamin K.

Fennel:

A plant with a licorice flavor, Fennel is used in a tea or chewed to relieve cough, sore-throat, aid digestion, offer relief to diarrhea. Fennel is a general treatment for colds. Fennel is also is used as a poultice for eye relief and headaches.

Feverfew:

Used to this day as a natural relief for fever and headaches, Feverfew is used to manage severe headaches like migraines. Feverfew also can be used for digestive problems, asthma, and muscle and joint pains.

Feverwort:

Another fever remedy that also is used for general pain; itching and joint stiffness is Feverwort. This herb can be ingested as a tea or chewed, or crushed to a paste as a salve or poultice.

Ginseng:

Ginseng is another contemporary herb that has a history that goes back across cultures for millennia. The roots were used by Native Americans as a food additive, a tea and a poultice to treat fatigue, boost energy, enhance the immune system and help with overall liver and lung function. The leaves and stems also were used, but the root has the most concentration of active ingredients.

Golden Seal:

Goldenseal is used for the common cold and other upper respiratory tract infections, as well as stuffy nose and hay fever. Some people use goldenseal for digestive disorders including stomach pain and swelling (gastritis), peptic ulcers, colitis, diarrhea, constipation, hemorrhoids, and intestinal gas.

Goldenseal is used for urinary tract infections (UTIs), internal bleeding, bleeding after childbirth, liver disorders, cancer, chronic fatigue syndrome (CFS), jaundice, gonorrhea, fever, pneumonia, malaria, whooping cough, and an eating disorder called anorexia.

Use goldenseal for vaginal pain and swelling and menstrual period problems.

Goldenseal is applied to the skin for rashes, ulcers, wound infections, itching, eczema, acne, dandruff, ringworm, herpes blisters, and cold sores. It is used as a mouthwash for sore gums and mouth.

Some people use goldenseal as an eyewash for eye inflammation and eye infections called conjunctivitis, or "pink eye."

Goldenseal is used in the ears for ringing, earache, and deafness.

Goldenseal is commonly found in the deep woods from Vermont to Arkansas and received its name from the golden-yellow scars on the base of the stem. When the stem is broken, the scar resembles a gold wax letter seal.

Goldenseal is effective for its use in masking illegal drugs in the urine. Goldenseal will cause false-negative results for marijuana, cocaine, amphetamines or numerous other illegal drugs.

Hops:

As a tea Hops is used to treat digestive problems and often mixed with other herbs or plants, such as aloe, to soothe muscles. Hops is also used to ease toothaches and relieve a sore throat.

Licorice:

Licorice roots and leaves can be used for coughs, colds, sore throats. The root can also be chewed to relieve toothaches. Licorice root has been known to treat diabetes and high blood pressure.

Mullein:

As an infusion in tea or added to a salad or other food, Mullein is a plant that has been used by Native Americans to treat inflammation, coughs and congestion and general lung afflictions. It is quite common and you probably have it growing in your backyard or somewhere close. Mullein, tobacco-like plant, is one of the oldest herbs, and some healers recommend inhaling the smoke from smoldering mullein roots and leaves to soothe asthma attacks and chest congestion. The roots can be made into a warm decoction for soaking swollen feet or reducing swelling in joints. Mullein also reduces swelling from inflammation and soothes painful, irritated tissue. It is particularly useful to the mucous membranes. A tea can be made from the flowers for a mild sedative.

Passion Flower:

The leaves and roots of Passion Flower are used to make a tea to treat anxiety and muscle pain. A poultice for injuries to the skin such as burns, insect bites and boils also can be made from Passion Flower.

Red Clover:

Red Clover grows everywhere and the flowers, leaves and roots are usually infused in a tea or are used to top food. It is used to manage inflammation, improve circulation and treat respiratory conditions. Red Clover is prescribed to help mothers produce more breast milk.

Rose Hip:

Rose Hip is the red to orange berry that is the fruit of wild roses. Rose Hip is already known to be a massive source of vitamin C. It can be eaten whole, crushed into a tea or added to food. This berry is used to treat colds and coughs, intestinal distress, as an antiseptic and to treat inflammation.

St. John's Wort:

Some of the most impressive health benefits of St. John's Wort include its ability to treat depression, improve mood swings, relieve anxiety, reduce the severity of pre-menstrual symptoms, ease addictive tendencies, regulate hormonal activity, protect against viral infections, reduce inflammation, and soothe the nervous system.

Valerian:
The Valerian root when used as an infusion in a tea relieves muscle aches, pain and is said to have a calming effect.

Willow Tree:
Willow bark refers to the bark from several varieties of the willow tree, including white willow or European willow, black willow or pussy willow, crack willow, purple willow, and others. The bark is used to make medicine. Willow bark acts a lot like aspirin, so it is used for pain, including headache, muscle pain, menstrual cramps, rheumatoid arthritis (RA), osteoarthritis, gout, and a disease of the spine called ankylosing spondylitis.

Willow bark's pain relieving potential has been recognized throughout history. Willow bark was commonly used during the time of Hippocrates, when people were advised to chew on the bark to relieve pain and fever.

Willow bark is also used to combat the common cold, flu, and weight loss.

"Let food be thy medicine, thy medicine shall be thy food". – Hippocrates

SUPPLEMENTS

The word "supplement" means exactly that: a nutrient or group of nutrients(vitamins, minerals, protein, carbohydrates, fats and oils) that are meant to supplement, but not substitute for a healthy diet that you eat on a regular basis.

Moringa Oleifera
Moringa is called "Nebedaye", which means "never die", in the African language of Wolof. It promises relief from many serious diseases and malfunctions that are very rampant in our society such as:

- Diabetes
- Complications leading to Kidney Diseases
- High Blood Pressure
- Stroke
- Heart Diseases
- Obesity brought on by malnutrition (overfed/ undernourished)
- Tumors & Cancer
- Lupus
- Arthritis & other Auto-Immune Diseases
- Glaucoma – Blindness
- Skin Diseases
- Prostate Enlargement & Prostate Cancer
- Hepatitis
- Chronic Fatigue Syndrome
- Irritable Bowel Syndrome

Additionally, Moringa has been clinically proven to bring relief from the ravages of HIV and AIDS. The seeds of Moringa purify water; this technology is currently being used for water purification in several major cities. Dr. Anthony Kweku Andoh, an Ethno-botanist from Ghana, West Africa, researched and taught about medicinal plants at the North Scale Institute, an educational, research and healing center just south of Atlanta, Georgia. He had studied the effects of Moringa since 2001. Moringa has hundreds of substances such as vitamins, enzymes, amino acids, fats, minerals, specific phyto-chemicals (plant-derived), each with clear importance and numerous applications in healing and nutrition. Dr. Andoh's extensive research and clinical trials using this plant establishes that it is so packed with nutrition it can be compared to few food supplements.

You can make a tea using the leaf or powdered form and sprinkle on your food.

Vitamin "C"
Vitamin C has been known to cure over 30 major diseases

including effectively reducing the symptoms of the common cold. There are some indicators that Vitamin C may also protect against cancers of the mouth and stomach. Use Ascorbic Acid (Vitamin C).

Here are some diseases that have been consistently cured with mega doses of Vitamin C: Scurvy, chicken pox, measles, mumps, tetanus and polio. While vaccines are now available for these illnesses, please remember this was not the case in the 1940's. Other diseases successfully treated with aggressive Vitamin C therapy: Pneumonia, encephalitis, herpes zoster, (shingles), herpes simplex, mononucleosis, pancreatitis, hepatitis, Rocky Mountain spotted fever, bladder infection, alcoholism and arthritis.

Vitamin C is remarkably safe even in enormously high doses. It does not cause kidney stones to form. In fact, it increases urine flow and favorably lowers the pH to help keep stones from forming.

"Cold Killer Tea"
One cup of Red Zinger Tea add
Juice of ½ medium size lemon
1 tsp honey
1 tbs raw apple cider vinegar
1 dash of cayenne pepper
Vitamin C liquid or powder 500 to 1000 mg.

Iron

Have you felt exhausted lately? Can you barely make it up the stairs without getting winded even though you're physically fit? If so, you might be lacking in iron -- especially if you're a woman.

Although many people don't think of iron as being a nutrient, you might be surprised to learn that low iron is the most common nutritional deficiency in the U.S. Almost 10% of women are iron deficient, according to figures from the Centers for Disease Control and Prevention.

Iron is an important component of hemoglobin, the substance in red blood cells that carries oxygen from your lungs to transport it throughout your body. Hemoglobin represents about two-thirds of the body's iron. If you don't have enough iron, your body can't make enough healthy oxygen-carrying red blood cells. A lack of red blood cells is called iron deficiency anemia. Without healthy red blood cells, your body can't get enough oxygen. If you're not getting sufficient oxygen in the body, you're going to become fatigued.

Dr. Sebi, a pathologist, herbalist, biochemist and naturalist offers an excellent Iron Supplement that offers enhanced iron-rich nourishment for the blood, brain and central nervous system.

REMEDIES FROM YOUR KITCHEN

Heal yourself at home with these foods found in most kitchens.

Honey and Cinnamon

Honey

Honey is produced in most of the countries of the world. Scientists of today also accept honey as a 'Ram Ban' (very effective) medicine for all kinds of diseases. Honey can be used without any side effects for any kind of diseases.

Today's nutritionists say that even though honey is sweet, if taken in the right dosage as a medicine, it does not harm diabetic patients.

In modern times, it has been discovered that honey has antibacterial properties and has other health benefits. Honey is composed of water, simple and complex sugars, minerals, enzymes, amino acids, and several different vitamins

Cinnamon

We find the evidence backed with research citations on why Cinnamon maybe the solution for Diabetes, Candida, Weight loss, Cancer, Alzheimer's, Toenail fungus, Parkinson's, Stomach flu and much more. The benefits of cinnamon are compelling.

Ceylon Cinnamon is particularly popular because it has low levels of Coumarin, a toxic, fragrant chemical compound commonly found in high concentration in Cassia Cinnamon. Coumarin, in high doses, can cause liver damage.

Ceylon Cinnamon is more effective in inhibiting bacterial growth.

Several studies have found that Cinnamon has properties that help those with insulin resistance. It is therefore very popular with Type 2 diabetics who take it to control their blood sugar levels.

Cinnamon has shown an amazing ability to stop medication-resistant yeast infections. This applies to Escherichia coli bacteria and Candida albicans fungus.

By far the best remedy for a horrible stomach bug is Cinnamon. It makes sense because Cinnamon is a powerful anti-bacterial.

As a digestive aid, cinnamon dramatically reduces the uncomfortable feelings associated with Irritable Bowel Syndrome (IBS) especially the bloating. It does this by killing bacteria and healing infections in the GI tract and enabling the gastric juices to work normally.

Uses for Honey and Cinnamon

A mixture of Honey and Cinnamon is believed to be a cure for a good number of diseases.

ARTHRITIS....

Arthritis patients may take daily, morning and night, one cup of hot water with two spoons of honey and one small teaspoon of cinnamon powder. If taken regularly even chronic arthritis may be cured. In a recent research study of 200 patients, it was found that when the doctors treated their patients with a mixture of one tablespoon Honey and half teaspoon Cinnamon powder before breakfast, within a week 73 of the patients were totally relieved of pain, and within a month, mostly all the patients who could not walk or move around because of arthritis started walking without pain.

BLADDER INFECTIONS...
Take two tablespoons of cinnamon powder and one teaspoon of honey in a glass of lukewarm water and drink it. It destroys the germs in the bladder.

CHOLESTEROL...
Two tablespoons of honey and three teaspoons of Cinnamon Powder mixed in 16 ounces of tea water given to a cholesterol patient, was found to reduce the level of cholesterol in the blood by 10 percent within two hours. If taken three times a day, any chronic cholesterol condition is cured. Pure honey taken with food daily relieves complaints of cholesterol.

FATIGUE...
Recent studies have shown that the sugar content of honey is more helpful rather than being detrimental to the strength of the body. Senior citizens, who take honey and cinnamon powder in equal parts, are more alert and flexible. A half tablespoon of honey taken in a glass of water and sprinkled with cinnamon powder, taken daily, in the morning and in the afternoon at about 3:00 P.M. when the vitality of the body starts to decrease, increases the vitality of the body within a week.

GAS...
When Honey is taken with cinnamon powder the stomach is relieved of gas.

HEART DISEASES...
Make a paste of honey and cinnamon powder, apply on bread, instead of jelly and jam, and eat it regularly for breakfast. It reduces the cholesterol in the arteries and saves you from heart attack. Regular use of this strengthens the heart beat. Various nursing homes have treated patients successfully and have found that as you age, the arteries and veins lose their flexibility and get clogged; honey and cinnamon revitalize the arteries and veins.

IMMUNE SYSTEM...
Daily use of honey and cinnamon powder strengthens the immune system and protects the body from bacterial and viral attacks. Scientists have found that honey has various vitamins and iron in large amounts. Constant use of Honey strengthens the white blood corpuscles to fight bacterial and viral diseases.

INDIGESTION...
Cinnamon powder sprinkled on two tablespoons of honey taken before food relieves acidity and digests the heaviest of meals.

PIMPLES...
Three tablespoons of honey and one teaspoon of cinnamon powder paste. Apply this paste on the pimples before sleeping and next morning wash it off with warm water. If done daily for two weeks, it removes pimples from the root.

SKIN INFECTIONS...
Applying honey and cinnamon powder in equal parts on the affected parts cures eczema, ringworm, and various other types of skin infections.

UPSET STOMACH...
Honey taken with cinnamon powder cures stomach ache and also clears stomach ulcers from the root.

WEIGHT LOSS...
Daily in the morning one half hour before breakfast on an empty stomach, and at night before sleeping, drink honey and cinnamon powder boiled in one cup of water. If taken regularly, it reduces the weight of even the most obese person. Also, drinking this mixture regularly does not allow the fat to accumulate in the body even though the person may eat a high calorie diet.

Vinegar (Apple Cider)

All vinegars contain an active ingredient known as acetic acid, which means all varieties (including pasteurized, unpasteurized, organic, and different flavors) are pretty much the same. Some personally prefer red wine vinegar over apple cider vinegar because it has a smoother taste. The only difference is that darker-colored vinegars may contain trace amounts of antioxidants found in dark colored fruits (like red grapes, pomegranate, etc.).

Multiple studies have shown a correlation between (Apple Cider) Vinegar and lower blood sugar levels. Its effects on blood sugar are similar to certain medications.

(Apple Cider) Vinegar's anti-glycemic effect is very well documented.

(Apple Cider) Vinegar blocks some of the digestion of starch. It doesn't block the starch 100%, but it definitely prevents at least some of the starch from being digested and raising your blood sugar. The acetic acid found in vinegar interferes with the enzymes in your stomach responsible for digesting starch so you can't absorb the calories from the carbs you've eaten.

Vinegar reduces bloating because it increases the acidity in the stomach, which allows you to digest the food you've eaten and helps the food to enter into the small intestine. Because slow digestion can cause acid reflux, a burning sensation that occurs when food in your stomach backs up all the way into your esophagus and triggers feelings of fullness, consuming vinegar to move things along can stop you from feeling bloated.

When your stomach isn't producing enough acid, this impairs the absorption of nutrients. You can help your body by ingesting a bit more acid in the form of vinegar, and you'll actually be able to use all the good stuff you consumed. In theory, this means that vinegar should help with weight loss, and existing research supports the notion. Consuming apple cider vinegar can help you feel more full, which can help you eat less.

Vinegar balances your body's pH levels, which could mean better bone health. Although vinegar is obviously acidic, it actually has a neutralizing effect once it's inside of you, meaning it makes your body's pH more basic (i.e., alkaline).

Blackstrap Molasses

Blackstrap Molasses has the lowest sugar content of any sugar cane product. The wonderment of Blackstrap Molasses is that it's unlike refined sugar, which has zero nutritional value. Blackstrap Molasses contains vital vitamins and minerals, such as iron, calcium, magnesium, vitamin B6, and selenium.

Blackstrap Molasses is a byproduct of sugar cane's refining process. Sugar cane is mashed to create juice, and then boiled once to create cane syrup. A second boiling creates molasses. After this syrup has been boiled a third time, a dark viscous liquid emerges known to Americans as Blackstrap Molasses.

Blackstrap Molasses is touted as a super food. It does have strong nutritional value with many benefits.

DIABETES-FRIENDLY SWEETENER...

If you have diabetes and a sweet tooth, you have a bit of a conundrum. While Blackstrap Molasses is derived from sugar and adds as many carbohydrates as other sugars, it may be digested more slowly, which may help stabilize blood sugar.

You can use Blackstrap Molasses in baking sweet treats. It's what gives gingerbread cookies their distinctive rich flavor.

BONE BOOSTER...

Everyone knows that calcium is needed for strong bones, but not everyone knows the importance that magnesium plays in growing them. Blackstrap Molasses contains both calcium and magnesium, so it can help you guard against osteoporosis.

About 5 tablespoons of blackstrap molasses contains 50 percent of the recommended daily allowance of calcium, 95 percent of iron, and 38 percent of magnesium. Proper levels of magnesium are also crucial in preventing diseases like osteoporosis and asthma along with others that can affect your blood and heart.

GOOD FOR THE BLOOD...

People with anemia — a condition where your body doesn't have enough red blood cells — often feel tired and weak. One type of anemia is caused by a lack of iron in the diet.

Blackstrap Molasses is a good source of iron. About 5 tablespoons of Blackstrap Molasses contains 95 percent of your daily allowance of iron.

Besides adding it into recipes, you can add it to hot water and drink warm or cold as a dietary supplement.

PACKED WITH POTASSIUM...

When it comes to potassium, Blackstrap Molasses is packed with the stuff. Try mixing blackstrap molasses in with baked beans, or even use it as a basting glaze on chicken, turkey, or other meats.

A spoonful of Blackstrap molasses straight can also give you a quick boost.

HAIR DE-FRIZZER...

Along with providing your body with important minerals, blackstrap molasses has been used to remove the frizziness in bleached, permed, or colored hair.

While pouring the sticky syrup directly into your hair is a pretty bad idea, it can be mixed with warm water and applied to the hair for 15 minutes. It can also be combined with other hair-healthy ingredients like your daily shampoo or coconut milk.

LAXATIVE QUALITIES...

Blackstrap Molasses is a natural stool softener that can improve the regularity and quality of your bowel movements

Additional mineral content of Blackstrap Molasses:

Two tablespoons of Blackstrap Molasses also contains 18 percent of our RDI (Recommended Daily Intake) of manganese (which helps produce energy from proteins and carbohydrates), 9.7 percent of our RDI of potassium (which plays an important role in nerve transmission and muscle contraction), 5 percent of our

RDI of vitamin B6 (which aids brain and skin development) and 3.4 percent of our RDI of selenium, an important antioxidant.

Cayenne

Capsaicin, the substance that gives Cayenne its spicy taste, is the active ingredient in many over-the-counter treatments for arthritis and muscle pain. Just a half of a teaspoon of Cayenne pepper along with a meal can help suppress appetite and burn calories. Capsaicin is a powerful decongestant. It stimulates the release of mucus from respiratory passages and opens your airways. Many published studies found that people with diabetes who ate a meal containing liberal amounts of chili pepper required less insulin to reduce their blood sugar afterward, which suggests the spice could have anti-diabetes benefits. The topical application of capsaicin in treating psoriasis has been evaluated. Researchers found that it significantly improved itching and other symptoms associated with psoriasis. Research also shows that capsaicin helps to lower blood pressure.

Black Cherry Juice

Drinking cherry juice is 'as good as' medication for high blood pressure. The anti-inflammatory and anti-oxidative properties of cherries juice could work wonders to help squelch the pain of gout. Studies show that cherry juice relieves aches and pains resulting from an intense workout or a pulled muscle and joint discomfort.

Garlic

Garlic has a variety of potent sulfur-containing compounds which are the reason for its characteristic pungent odor.

Allicin, the vital compound in the pod, is known to have great anti-bacterial, anti-viral, anti-fungal and anti-oxidant properties. Garlic is best when it's finely chopped, minced or pureed and left to sit for some time.

Garlic is also a reliable source of selenium.

Allicin along with other compounds also has a healing effect on your circulatory, digestive and immunological systems and helps in lowering blood pressure and detoxification. The compounds help control bacterial, viral, fungal, yeast and worm infestations.

Fresh garlic is thought to play a role in preventing food poisoning by killing bacteria like E. coli and Salmonella.

Ginger
DIGESTIVE ISSUES...

Ginger has a long history of use for relieving digestive problems such as nausea, loss of appetite, motion sickness and pain. The root or underground stem (rhizome) of the ginger plant can be consumed fresh, powdered, dried as a spice, in oil form or as juice.

The phenolic compounds in ginger are known to help relieve gastrointestinal irritation, stimulate saliva and bile production and suppress gastric contractions and movement of food and fluids through the Gastro-intestinal tract.

NAUSEA...

Chewing raw Ginger or drinking ginger tea is a common home remedy for nausea during cancer treatment.

Ginger tea can help relieve nausea and aid cold recovery.

Pregnant women experiencing morning sickness can safely use Ginger to relieve nausea and vomiting, often in the form of ginger lozenges or candies.

During cold weather, drinking ginger tea is a good way to keep warm. It is diaphoretic, which means that it promotes sweating, working to warm the body from within. As such, in the wake of a cold, ginger tea is particularly useful.

To make ginger tea at home, slice parts of fresh Ginger and steep in a cup of hot water. Adding a slice of lemon or a drop of honey adds flavor and additional benefits, including vitamin C and antibacterial properties.

PAIN REDUCTION...

A daily ginger supplementation reduced exercise-induced muscle pain by 25%.

Ginger has also been found to reduce the symptoms of dysmenorrhea (severe pain during a menstrual cycle). In one study, 83% of women taking ginger capsules reported improvements in pain symptoms compared to 47% of those on placebo.

INFLAMMATION...
Ginger has been used for centuries to reduce inflammation and treat inflammatory conditions.

A study published found ginger root supplement administered to volunteer participants reduced inflammation markers in the colon within a month. Researchers on the study explained that by decreasing inflammation, the risk of colon cancer is also likely to decrease. Ginger has also shown promise in clinical trials for treating inflammation associated with osteoarthritis.

Lemons

Lemons are alkalizing for the body. Lemons are acidic to begin with but they are alkaline-forming on body fluids helping to restore balance to the body's pH.

Lemons are rich in vitamin C and flavonoids that work against infections like the flu and colds.

Your liver loves lemons. "The lemon is a wonderful stimulant to the liver and is a dissolvent of uric acid and other poisons. Lemons liquefy the bile," says Jethro Kloss in his book *Back to Eden*. Fresh lemon juice added to a large glass of water in the morning is a great liver detoxifier.

Lemons increase peristalsis in the bowels, helping to create a bowel movement thus eliminating waste and helping with regularity.

The citric acid in lemon juice helps to dissolve gallstones, calcium deposits, and kidney stones.

Grapefruit

Grapefruit has copious amounts of vitamin C which helps prevent or fight the common cold.. Grapefruit also combat free radicals that can wreak havoc in the body. Cancer, stroke, and heart attack may all be related to unchecked free radicals.

Kidney Stone Prevention...
Kidney stones are usually a buildup of calcium, once developed these stones must either pass through the urethra or be broken up medically. Anyone who has had a kidney stone can relate to their extremely painful condition. The greatest benefit and prevention of developing kidney stones can be reaped through drinking up to a liter of grapefruit juice daily.

Natural Fat Burner...
Grapefruit that burns fat is not a simple rumor or fad. Scientific research reveals the amazing power of this wonderful breakfast or anytime fruit. Simply enjoy a glass of grapefruit juice or half of a grapefruit before each meal to reap the benefits.

Charge Up Your Metabolism...
Grapefruit also speeds up your metabolism, supporting your efforts to lose weight. Along with proper diet and exercise, a boost in your metabolism can help you lose up to two pounds a week. An added benefit of a raised metabolism is that fat continues to burn even as you rest. Pounds can be lost even faster and a healthier weight is maintained far more easily.

Liver Cleanser...
Grapefruit helps the liver by cleansing unhealthy toxins from the body. Detoxification of the liver is said to improve and help alleviate symptoms of chronic conditions, such as, depression, stiff muscles, and chronic headaches. Dangerous toxins that affect our health are all around us, a Grapefruit cleansing can help eliminate some of these deadly toxins.

Protection Against Prostate Cancer...

Rich in antioxidants that attack carcinogens that lurk in the prostate is another benefit of consuming Grapefruit. Research appears to indicate that the fruit even repairs damaged cells at the DNA level. Enjoy regularly with a healthy diet to combat and prevent this disease.

Gum Disease...

Scientists have found that eating two Grapefruit a day prevents and can reverse damage caused by gum disease. The conclusion was that free radicals are not formed when grapefruit is added to the diet. Left untreated or undiagnosed gum disease can lead to oral cancer. Gum disease can also lead to bacteria that damages the heart.

Sea Salt for Dry Skin

You don't need an expensive skincare product to treat rough patches on your knees, elbows, and heels. A sea salt scrub made at home will work just as well. Mix sea salt with olive oil or coconut oil.

Oatmeal for eczema

Calm itchy, inflamed skin using this breakfast food. Oatmeal soothes rashes because it's packed with phytochemicals that have anti-inflammatory properties. Create a soothing bath by grinding 1/3 cup of plain oatmeal (no flavors!) into a fine powder using your blender; pour the powder into lukewarm water and stir in evenly with your hands until the water is a milky color. Bathe for 20 minutes.

Prunes for Constipation

Dried plums are rich in insoluble fiber, a key nutrient to help fight constipation. "Insoluble fiber doesn't dissolve in water and creates more bulk so waste can push through the digestive system.

SPICE IT UP

A spice is a substance (such as pepper or nutmeg) that is used in cooking to add flavor to food and that comes from a dried plant and is usually a powder or seed. Each spice listed also has specific medicinal properties. It might be noted that specific spices affect body types differently.

Basil

Basil is mentioned in scriptures as a gift for humankind from heaven. Its medicinal properties include:
- Tonic
- Antidepressant
- Antiseptic
- Expectorant

Cumin

The health benefits of cumin include its ability to aid in digestion, improve immunity and treat piles, insomnia, respiratory disorders, asthma, bronchitis, common cold, anemia and boils. Cumin is a member of the family of herbs including caraway, parsley, and dill. The benefits of consuming cumin include:
- Antiflatulant
- Mild Stimulant
- Antispasmadic
- Antioxidant

Cumin is used and actually advised by pediatricians to be used to wean children off the bottle.

Marjoram

This is a plant of the Mediterranean region that has been well known and respected for its medicinal uses for many years. Marjoram reduces the pain associated with colds, fevers, inflammation, overexertion of muscles, toothaches. The best thing about this and other herbs is that they do not have any adverse side effects, unlike the other analgesic pain relievers available on the market.

Some herbalists use Marjoram to treat a variety of ailments including:
- Relief from menstruation pain
- Colds, coughs
- Ear pain
- Aromatic agent in soaps and cosmetic products

Rosemary

Rosemary was used in ancient times to treat forgetfulness. It is used as a tonic, general stimulant and is used to induce vitality. Rosemary helps with:
- Digestion
- Promotes sweating
- Induces bile flow

Thyme

Thyme is believed to be an aphrodisiac. Studies show it has powerful anti microbial affects against Salmonella and E. Coli. The flowers, leaves and oil of thyme are commonly used by people for the treatment of bedwetting, diarrhea, stomach ache, arthritis, colic, sore throat, cough (including whooping cough), bronchitis, flatulence and as a diuretic (to increase urination) A delicate looking herb with a penetrating fragrance, thyme is an herb we should all take time to investigate and enjoy. And with about sixty different varieties including French (common) thyme, lemon thyme, orange thyme and silver thyme, this herb is sure to add some spice to your life.

Turmeric

Turmeric is a spice that comes from the turmeric plant. It is commonly used in Asian food. You probably know Turmeric as the main spice in curry. It contains a yellow-colored chemical called curcumin, which is often used to color foods and cosmetics. It has a warm, bitter taste and is frequently used to flavor or color curry powders, mustards, butters, and cheeses. But the root of Turmeric is also widely used to make medicine.

Turmeric is used for arthritis, heartburn, joint pain, stomach pain, Crohn's disease, ulcerative colitis, hemorrhaging, diarrhea, intestinal gas, stomach bloating, loss of appetite, jaundice, liver problems, infection, stomach ulcers, irritable bowel syndrome (IBS), gallbladder disorders, high cholesterol, a skin conditions and inflammation from radiation treatment.

Turmeric is also used for headaches, bronchitis, colds, lung infections, fibromyalgia, leprosy, fever, menstrual problems, itchy skin and fatigue.

Some people apply turmeric to the skin for joint pain, ringworm, sprains and swellings, bruising, leech bites, eye infections, acne, soreness inside of the mouth, infected wounds, and gum disease.

Ayurveda

Ayurveda is a traditional healing system originated in India approximately 6,000 years ago. In Sanskrit, Ayu means "Life" and Veda means "knowledge or science". Ayurveda can be interpreted as the Science of Life. This "Science of Life" is a holistic healing system, which is designed to promote good health and longevity rather than curing a disease.

Holistic treatment is the hallmark of treatment in Ayurveda. It demands that one herb or one drug would not cure the imbalance. Therefore, traditionally, in most of the cases, a combination of herbs and plants (which are even part of staple food) are recommended for treatment.

Oil Pulling

Used primarily in Ayurvedic medicine, oil pulling is a fantastic oral detoxification procedure that is simply done by swishing a tablespoon of oil (typically coconut oil, olive or sesame oil) in your mouth for 10-20 minutes.

Oil pulling is one of the best ways to remove bacteria from the mouth and promote healthy teeth and gums!

It has taken quite some time, but oil pulling has finally gained some popularity in the United States.

Ayurveda advises oil gargling and swishing to purify the entire system; as it holds that each section of the tongue is connected to different organ such as to the kidneys, lungs, liver, heart, small intestines, stomach, colon, and spine, similarly to reflexology and TCM (Traditional Chinese Medicine).

Worst Foods to Consume

Sugar

We are all eating sugar in unprecedented amounts, often without even knowing it; and it's doing far worse things in our bodies than just making us fat... though it's definitely doing that, too, says Dr. Amy Lee. Dr. Lee is an American Board of Internal Medicine Physician, Nutrition Specialists and registered with the American Board of Obesity Medicine. She lectures on "Exposing Sugar for What It Is". "Sugar is the most dangerous toxin of our time".

The scientific and medical studies support a role for sugar in the epidemics of metabolic syndrome, cardiovascular disease, and type 2 diabetes.

The tides have finally shifted. Sugar — in all its forms, including high-fructose corn syrup — is now being called out for the poison it is.

You won't find this stuff anywhere in nature. *And yet you're likely eating it at every meal.*

The typical American now swallows the equivalent of 22 sugar cubes every 24 hours. That means the average person eats 70 pounds of straight sugar every year. In case you're wondering, it should be no more than five percent of your diet, or about six teaspoons of the sweet stuff per day, per the World Health Organization.

A recent study suggests that sugary foods/pastries could be as addictive as cocaine or morphine. When scientists scanned the brains of subjects who'd just eaten a high-sugar treat, everyone's nucleus accumbens—the part of the brain that switches on when a person shoots heroin or smokes crack—was lit up like fireworks. By contrast, the control group that swallowed low-sugar treats had no nucleus accumbens activity.

The process that turns sugar canes into white, granulated crystals is an extensive operation that involves multiple rounds of high-temperature treatment, evaporation, filtering, and spinning. Not to mention, industrial chemicals like sulfur dioxide that are bubbled through the sugar to bleach it.

Before sugar enters the bloodstream from the digestive tract, it is broken down into two simple sugars... glucose and fructose.

Glucose is found in every living cell on the planet. If we don't get it from the diet, our bodies produce it. Glucose is a molecule absolutely vital to life.

Fructose is different. Our bodies do not produce it in any significant amount and there is no physiological need for it. Humans don't produce fructose and throughout history have never consumed it except seasonally when fruit were ripe. Thirty Percent of the fructose you consume becomes fat in your body.

Glucose and fructose are metabolized very differently by the body. The thing with fructose is that it can only be metabolized by the liver in any significant amounts.

This is not a problem if we eat a little bit (such as from fruit) or we just finished an exercise session. In this case, the fructose will be turned into glycogen and stored in the liver until we need it.

High Fructose Corn Syrup

As part of the chemical process used to make high fructose corn syrup, the glucose and fructose — which are naturally bound together — become separated. This allows the fructose to mainline directly into your liver, which turns on a factory of fat production in your liver.

This leads to fatty liver, a common disease in America today, affecting 90 million Americans. This, in turn, leads to Diabetes — Pre-Diabetes and Type 2 Diabetes. High fructose corn syrup is the real driver of the current epidemic of heart attacks, strokes, cancer, dementia, and of course, Type 2 diabetes.

You see, fructose messes up two things your brain uses to regulate your eating:[73]

1. It blinds your brain to leptin, the hormone that makes you feel full.
2. It fails to stop ghrelin, the hormone that makes you feel hungry.

We are eating huge doses of high fructose corn syrup. It is sweeter and cheaper than regular sugar and is in every processed food and sugar-sweetened drink. Purging it from your diet is the single best thing you can do for your health!

The average 20-ounce soda contains 15 teaspoons of sugar, all of it high fructose corn syrup. And when you eat sugar in those doses, it becomes a toxin. *HFCS contains dangerous chemicals and contaminants*

If you want to stay healthy, lose weight easily, get rid of chronic disease, and help reduce the obesity epidemic, the single most important thing you can do is eliminate high fructose corn syrup from your diet and from your children's diet. Just banish it from your house

While eliminating HFCS from your diet is difficult, it can be done. And in the process you may just find that you're eating more

The Wonders of Natural Healing

"real food". "Real food" means food with real ingredients, food that can stand the test of label-reading scrutiny, food that your grandmother would have eaten. The best sugar is date palm sugar.

Here are five ways you can keep high fructose corn syrup out of your diet:

1. Buy organic varieties of certain foods

There's an easy way to bring some organic foods into your life and at the same time avoid HFCS.

Just like in the good old days when ketchup, rolls, mustard, salad dressings, jam, and hundreds of other processed food items didn't contain this test-tube sweetener, organic foods do not contain HFCS.

Swap out some conventional condiments, breads and crackers for organic ones and you'll get an "easy pass" to faster HFCS-free shopping.

2. Shop at a Whole Foods Market

Whole Foods Market, the entire store, is an HFCS-free zone!

High fructose corn syrup is on the Whole Foods Market list of "unacceptable ingredients for food," a list that also includes such chemical additives as artificial colors and flavors, aspartame and bromated flour.

3. Steer clear of fast-food restaurants

Fast food places are hotbeds of bad ingredients – including, of course, high fructose corn syrup. Buns, dressings, drinks, condiments and sauces are likely culprits, but so are items such as cole slaw and potato salad and even many so-called "healthier choices" such as carrot salad and sliced fruits.

4. Eat more "food" and fewer "food products"

A ready-made meal (actually called a "TV dinner" when it was first introduced by Swanson in the early 1950s), is convenient but comes at a cost, and if you're trying to cut HFCS out of your diet, this is a very good place to start.

Author Michael Pollan says in his book "In Defense of Food," that long lists of ingredients that are "unfamiliar, unpronounceable," and "more than five in number or that include high fructose corn syrup," are "reliable markers" that the foods you are considering consuming have crossed the line from "foods to food products."

5. Read the ingredient label before the item goes in your cart
Once something hits your shopping cart, it's pretty much a done deal, so make your decisions carefully before that fateful moment. Despite what may seem like a bounty of delicious, healthy foods, supermarkets are stocked with scores of salt, fat and chemical-laden products, including loads of items containing HFCS.

Fat, Salt and Sugar Alter Brain Chemistry

Make Us Eat Junk Food

The career path of David A. Kessler, the Harvard-trained doctor, lawyer, medical school dean and former commissioner of the Food and Drug Administration, was on a mission to understand a problem that has vexed him since childhood: why he can't resist certain foods.

His resulting theory, described in his new book, "The End of Overeating," is startling. Foods high in fat, salt and sugar alter the brain's chemistry in ways that compel people to overeat. "Much of the scientific research around overeating has been physiology -- what's going on in our body," he said. "The real question is what's going on in our brain."

The labels showed the foods we eat at fast food restaurants were bathed in salt, fat and sugars, beyond what a diner might expect by reading the menu, Kessler said. The ingredient list for Southwestern Eggrolls mentioned salt eight different times; sugars showed up five times. The "egg rolls," which are deep-fried in fat, contain chicken that has been chopped up like meatloaf to give it a "melt in the mouth" quality that also makes it faster to eat. By the time a diner has finished this appetizer, she has consumed 910 calories, 57 grams of fat and 1,960 milligrams of sodium.

"Instead of satisfying hunger, the salt-fat-sugar combination will stimulate the brain to crave more", Kessler said. For many, the come-on offered by Lay's Potato Chips -- "Betcha can't eat just one" -- is scientifically accurate. And the food industry manipulates this neurological response, designing foods to induce people to eat more than they should or even want, Kessler found.

"Highly palatable" foods -- those containing fat, sugar and salt -- stimulate the brain to release dopamine, the neurotransmitter associated with the pleasure center, he found. In time, the brain gets wired so that dopamine pathways light up at the mere suggestion of the food, such as driving past a fast-food restaurant, and the urge to eat the food grows insistent. Once the food is eaten, the brain releases opioids, which bring emotional relief. Together, dopamine and opioids create a pathway that can activate every time a person is reminded about the particular food. This happens regardless of whether the person is hungry. They are manipulating consumer behavior to sell products that can harm health", he said.

International Flavors and Fragrances, Inc.

International Flavors & Fragrances, Inc. engages in the creation, manufacture, and supply of flavors and fragrances that are used in the food, beverage, personal care, and household products industries. It creates new smells in pilot kitchens. It comes up with the flavors and smells for ice cream, sweets, toothpaste, popular soft drinks, sports drinks, bottled teas, wine coolers, for all-natural drinks, soy drinks and Fast Foods.

The Food and Drug Administration does not require flavor

companies to disclose the ingredients of their additives, so long as the chemicals are considered by the agency to be GRAS (Generally Regarded As Safe). This lack of public disclosure enables the companies to maintain the secrecy of their formulas.

The small elite group of scientists who create most of the flavors in most of the food now consumed in the United States are called "flavorists."

The job of the flavorist is to conjure illusions about processed foods, including fast food, to ensure consumer likeability. A typical artificial strawberry flavor like the kind found in a fast food strawberry milkshake may contain over 38 chemicals to artificially produce the taste of strawberry.

Alkaline Water

The "alkaline" in alkaline water refers to its pH level. A measure of acidity or alkalinity of water soluble substances (**pH stands** for 'potential of Hydrogen'). A **pH** value is a number from 1 to 14, with 7 as the middle (neutral) point. Values below 7 indicate acidity which increases as the number decreases, 1 being the most acidic. The cells and fluids in most people's bodies are overly acidic. This can cause a lot of health problems. It prevents your body from neutralizing and disposing of harmful poisonous toxins and leaves you more susceptible to the cell damaging free radical oxidation that leads to cancer and other diseases."

On top of soothing acid reflux, other benefits of alkaline water, are that it helps neutralize acid in the bloodstream, which leads to increased oxygen levels and improved energy and metabolism; it contains antioxidant properties (anti-aging and anti-disease); and cleanses the colon.

Excessively acidic pH can lead to many serious health problems such as cancer, cardiovascular disease, diabetes, osteoporosis and heartburn. If you keep your body in an acidic state for a long period of time, it can drastically accelerate aging. Robert O. Young, in The pH Miracle, says, that most health problems arise from being acidic. This is because parasites, bad bacteria, viruses, and candida overgrowth thrive in acidic environments. But an alkaline environment neutralizes bacteria and other pathogens.

Therefore, maintaining pH balance is one of the important tools to optimizing your health.

Cupping

Cupping Therapy has been around for thousands of years. It developed over time from the original use of hollowed out animal horns (the Horn Method) to treat boils and suck out the toxins out of snakebites and skin lesions. Horns slowly evolved into bamboo cups, which were eventually replaced by glass.

The true origin of cupping still remains uncertain to this day. Some consider the Chinese to be responsible for cupping, however, the earliest pictorial records date back to the ancient Egyptians around 1500 B.C. Translations of hieroglyphics in the Ebers Papyrus, the oldest medical text book, detail the use of cupping for treating fever, pain, vertigo, menstrual imbalances, weakened appetite and helping to accelerate the healing crisis.

Breathing

What is Breathing

Breathing is the air taken into or expelled from the lungs. Breathing is the process that moves air in and out of the lungs, or oxygen through other respiratory organs. It is one part of physiological respiration required to sustain life.

If the air cells of the lungs were spread out over an unbroken surface, they would cover an area of fourteen thousand feet. The air is drawn into the lungs by the action of the diaphragm, a great strong, flat sheet-like muscle, stretched across the chest, separating the chest-box from the abdomen. The diaphragm's action is almost as automatic as that of the heart, although it may be transformed into a semi-voluntary muscle by an effort of the will. When it expands, it increases the size of the chest and lungs, and the air rushes into the vacuum thus created. When it relaxes the chest and lungs contract and the air is expelled from the lungs.

Breath is essential to life. It is the first thing we do when we are born and the last thing we do when we are pronounced dead.

When you experience stressful thoughts, your sympathetic nervous system triggers the body's ancient fight-or-flight response, giving you a burst of energy to respond to the perceived danger. Your breathing becomes shallow and rapid, and you primarily breathe from the chest and not the lower lungs. This can make you feel short of breath, which is a common symptom when you feel anxious or frustrated. At the same time, your body produces a surge of hormones such as cortisol and epinephrine (also known as adrenaline), which increase your blood pressure and pulse rate and put you in a revved up state of high alert.

With deep breathing, you can reverse these symptoms instantly and create a sense of calm in your mind and body. When you breathe deeply and slowly, you activate the parasympathetic nervous system, which reverses the stress response in your body. Deep breathing stimulates the main nerve in the parasympathetic nervous system—the vagus nerve—slowing down your heart rate, lowering your blood pressure, and calming your body and mind.

In addition, with deep breathing, you engage the abdominal muscles and diaphragm instead of just the muscles in the upper chest and neck. This conditioning of the respiratory muscles results in improved efficiency of oxygen exchange with every breath by allowing more air exchange to occur in the lower lungs. It also reduces strain on the muscles of the neck and upper chest, allowing these muscles to relax. Deep breathing is more relaxing and efficient for the body, allowing higher volumes of oxygen to reach the body's cells and tissues.

As well as reversing the physical stress response in the body, deep breathing can help calm and slow down the emotional turbulence in the mind. Breathing can have an immediate effect on diffusing emotional energy so there is less reactivity to our emotions.

Benefits of Proper Deep Breathing:

- Lowers your heart rate
- Lowers blood pressure and cardiac output
- Increases blood oxygen levels
- Promotes clearer thinking
- Relieves stress
- Increases metabolism
- Improves circulation
- Supports detoxification
- Reduces attention deficit and hyperactivity

Here are some general rules for more efficient breathing:
- Breathe through the nose as much as possible. The nose pre-warms, moistens, and filters the air before it reaches the lungs.
- Stand erect with your hands to the side. Begin to inhale slowly and concentrate on allowing the air to fill the lower portion of your lungs first. To do this you must relax your abdominal, or stomach muscles.
- While still inhaling, let the air fill the middle portion of the lungs as you let the rib cage relax and expand.
- Continue inhaling as the upper part of the lungs fill. As this happens, gently raise your collarbone and pull your shoulders up and back.
- Now exhale reversing the above sequence—that is, let the air release from the upper lungs by relaxing the collarbone and shoulders, then the middle portion of the lungs, and so forth.
- Make sure your breaths are even, and visualize each section of the lungs completely filling with air. As you fill the upper portion of the lungs, picture your chest expanding and your shoulders becoming more erect and higher.

Sun Gazing

The practice of sun gazing has existed as long as humans have occupied planet Earth. The power of the sun, in principle, can awaken inherent gifts and powers within us to higher levels – in essence raising our frequency- and our ability to manifest.

Sun energy is a power source that activates the brain through the eyes—the eyes act as a doorway.

Safe sun gazing does not harm the eyes – it makes eyes healthier. Sun gazing practices of the Mayans, Egyptians and Incan priests/priestesses, Native Americans and monks serve to remind us of this truth

Fact: Safest time to sun gaze – first hour of sunrise, within one hour of sunset.

Sun gazing is a one-time practice that is typically done over a 9 month period in 3 phases (depending on the climate in your area)

Phase I (0-3 months)
Day one – look at the sun for a maximum of 10 seconds (during first hour of sunrise)
Day two – look the rising sun for 20 seconds and then add 10 seconds each day thereafter. Eye stillness and steadiness are not required; do not wear lenses or glasses while sun gazing.
Make sure to stand in bare foot on bare earth or sand (not grass). As a precaution, have your eyes examined before you consider sun gazing. If your cheeks get heated up- stop sun gazing. Listen to your body!

Phase II (3-6 months)
When you reach 30 minutes duration of looking at the sun— you will slowly be liberated from certain physical imbalances, illness and diseases- as all the colors of the sun will have reached the brain through the eyes. The brain redirects the flow of color prana appropriately throughout your body – where it's needed. The vital organs are dependent on certain sun color prana. For instance- Kidney = red; Heart = yellow; Liver = green, etc. This color prana reaches the organs and corrects deficiencies and imbalances/and/

or weaknesses—this is how color therapy works! At this phase your appetite for food will lessen.

Phase III (6-9 months)
The absorption of sun energy becomes your new food! Need for food intake will decrease substantially – as you feel less hungry .Remember food is not necessary for the body to function – only energy! By eight months the concept of hunger will no longer exist. All mechanisms associated with hunger like aroma, cravings and hunger pangs will also disappear. At 9 months you will reach a total of 44 minutes of sun gazing – and that is the maximum daily intake recommended by solar science to ensure proper eye care.

Benefits of Sun Gazing

- Activates areas of the brain that are currently dormant by activating the hypothalamus.
- Supplies vitamins A and D during the first hour of sunrise
- Brings balance to the mind; encourages a positive mind set
- Increases confidence
- Further develops powers that are already inherent within you
- Problem solving becomes easier – with increased brain function, comprehension, and heightened intuition
- Strengthens the hypothalamus tract – which acts as a critical link between the nervous system and the endocrine system via the pituitary gland
- Decreases appetite for traditional food, coupled with increase energy levels.

Mac's Home Remedies

Eliminates most symptoms of cold and flu:
1. Mix 1.10 teaspoon Cayenne pepper in 16 oz med hot water, squeeze ½ lemon and honey to taste. Drink this solution all day until you feel better.

Rids Congestion:
2. 8 oz of hot water, add 6-7 drops of peppermint oil. Mix well and drink all within a few minutes.

Eliminates headaches:
3. Add a couple of drops of peppermint oil in hand, massage with forefingers into both temples.

Helps to relieve a sore throat:
4. Take a small damp cloth that will fit around your neck, put in freezer. Put a small towel around the damp frozen cloth, wrap securely around your neck. Wear for 20 minutes. Repeat of necessary

Breaks up congestion:
5. Take as much as 1,000 – 5,000 mg of niacin. Let your body be the judge of quantity. The body will expel large amounts of mucous from the nose.

Improves memory:
6. Pull on the bottom portion of your ears every day.

Stimulates brain activity:
7. Use the tips of your fingers to tap all over your head.

Pulls toxins or infection out of areas of the body:
8. Cut strips of wool or cotton fleece, soak in castor oil, wrap around area, you may need to wrap plastic around the bandages so oil will not stain clothes or bed sheets. It is best to wear at night and remove in the morning.

The Wonders of Natural Healing

Soothes overstressed and overstrained eyes:
9. Make separate bowls of hot and ice water, alternate hot and cold cloth over eyes for 1 min each.

Strengthens the eyes, improves vision:
10. Blink eyes slowly for 1 min. Blink fast for 1 min. squeeze eyes shut and open repeatedly for 1 min. Works best after doing above hot/cold therapy.

Stops heart attack:
11. Mix solution of cayenne pepper and water in small bottle, with an aspirator, spray in the face.

Stops asthma attack:
12. Rub peppermint oil all over chest, throat and inhale repeatedly.

Relaxes sore tight muscles:
13. Soak in hot tub of Epson Salt

Stops abscess pain:
14. Pack cayenne pepper into a hurting or abscessed tooth.

Stops diarrhea:
15. Eat a cucumber with ½ pint of nonfat yogurt.

Pin Worm treatment:.
16. Garlic
    Mince 2 or 3 cloves of fresh garlic
    Wrap in bread and eat at night

17. Turpentine and Sugar
    Take several drops of turpentine on a teaspoonful of sugar, followed-up with a tablespoonful of Castor oil. Drink lots of fluids throughout the day. This remedy is known to cure Candida and eliminate pin worms.

Hippocrates - *"A wise man should consider that health is the greatest of human blessings"*.

About the Author

Hajar Young is owner of the Stress Management Consulting firm, Hajar Natural Healing. She employs her own stress relief technique, "The Hajdrianne Technique". Visit her website at www.hajarnaturalhealing.com.

You can book Ms. Young for corporate events, conferences, workshops, individual stress relief sessions by calling 404-438-1991.

Hajar Young is a North Carolina native, a travel enthusiast and certified Words with Friends addict who for the past 20 years has worked in the Healing Arts. She is knowledgeable, conscientious, and passionate about the work she does.... She is a modern day woman, an activist and a celebrated Healer.

Educated at New Jersey City University where she received her BS in Business Administration. She is mother to three successful, beautiful and prosperous contributors to society and grandmother to eight.

Giving back is her personal solution to living a successful life. She is founder and CEO of Yes, Inc. a 501 (C) 3 nonprofit organization whose mission is to provide basic human necessities to those in need. The organization's motto is, "Want for your brother what you want for yourself". Visit us at www.yesshoesinc.org.

The Wonders of Natural Healing

Her Personal Movement is Towards a Better World

Love all and hate none.
Mere talk of peace will avail you naught.
Mere talk of God and religion will not take you far.
Bring out all the latent powers of your being and
Reveal the full magnificence of your immortal self.
Be surcharged with peace and joy, and scatter
them wherever you are and wherever you go.
Be a blazing fire of truth; be a beauteous blossom
of love; and be a soothing balm of peace.
With your spiritual light, dispel the darkness of
ignorance; dissolve the clouds of discord and war,
and spread goodwill, peace and harmony among
the people. Never seek any help, charity or favors
from anybody except God. Never go to the courts
of kings and rulers, but never refuse to bless
and help the needy and the poor, the widow
and the orphan, if they come to your door.
This is your Mission of Peace, to serve the people...
Carry it out dutifully and courageously.

By Khwaja Muinuddin Chishti.

www.ingramcontent.com/pod-product-compliance
Lightning Source LLC
Chambersburg PA
CBHW071544080526
44588CB00011B/1780